D-Day

PETER BENOIT

Children's Press®
An Imprint of Scholastic Inc.
New York   Toronto   London   Auckland   Sydney
Mexico City   New Delhi   Hong Kong
Danbury, Connecticut

Content Consultant
James Marten, PhD
Professor and Chair, History Department
Marquette University, Milwaukee, Wisconsin

Library of Congress Cataloging-in-Publication Data
Benoit, Peter, 1955–
 D-Day / by Peter Benoit.
   pages cm. — (A true book)
Includes bibliographical references and index.
ISBN 978-0-531-20498-6 (lib. bdg.) — ISBN 978-0-531-21733-7 (pbk.)
1. World War, 1939–1945—Campaigns—France—Normandy—Juvenile literature. I. Title.
D756.5.N6B442 2014
940.54'21421—dc23   2014003934

All rights reserved. Published in 2015 by Children's Press, an imprint of Scholastic Inc.
Printed in the United States of America 113
SCHOLASTIC, CHILDREN'S PRESS, A TRUE BOOK™, and associated logos are trademarks and/or registered trademarks of Scholastic Inc.

1 2 3 4 5 6 7 8 9 10 R 24 23 22 21 20 19 18 17 16 15

Front cover: U.S. troops arriving at the beaches of Normandy a few days after D-Day

Back cover: U.S. glider troops on parade before D-Day.

Find the Truth!

Everything you are about to read is true *except* for one of the sentences on this page.

Which one is **TRUE**?

Some Allied troops carried bicycles when they invaded Normandy.

The invasion of Normandy began at noon on June 6, 1944.

Find the answers in this book.

Contents

THE BIG TRUTH!

General Dwight Eisenhower and Field Marshal Bernard Montgomery discuss invasion plans.

American soldiers celebrate victory in Paris outside Notre Dame Cathedral.

A German soldier prepares to throw a hand grenade during the invasion of Poland.

Europe at War

World War II began in Europe when Germany invaded Poland on September 1, 1939. The invasion caused Great Britain and France to declare war on Germany. They promised to help defend Poland. Great Britain, France, and Poland became known as the Allies. However, Poland was just a first step for Germany. German leader Adolf Hitler planned to take over the rest of Europe as well.

Roughly 1.5 million German soldiers invaded the Soviet Union in 1939.

Occupied Europe

The German military was fast and effective. The Germans invaded Denmark and Norway in April 1940. Denmark **surrendered** immediately, while Norway fought for two months. By the end of May, Germany also occupied Luxembourg, the Netherlands, and Belgium. German tanks rolled into Paris, France, on June 14, 1940. Allied soldiers were forced to flee from German-occupied France to Britain. A year later, Germany invaded the Soviet Union to the east.

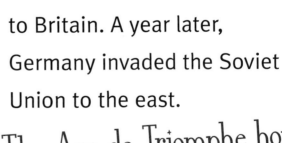

The Arc de Triomphe honors the 1805 French victory over Austria and Russia in the Battle of Austerlitz.

German troops march through the Arc de Triomphe in Paris, France.

Members of a special German force called the SS organize Jewish people before sending them by train to concentration camps or other destinations.

The German military claimed most of the food and other resources in areas it occupied. This led to shortages for the rest of the population. Certain groups of people suffered extreme forms of cruel treatment. Russians and Polish people were forced into slave labor. Educated people, such as teachers and priests, were often killed to keep them from convincing others to fight against Germany. Jewish people across Europe were sent to **concentration camps**. Many people fled to unoccupied regions.

German officials inspect wooden obstacles constructed on beaches as part of the Atlantic Wall.

Constructing a Defense

Germany wanted to protect its new territories from any possible Allied invasion. The German military began building a chain of **fortifications** along Europe's northern coast. It included large cannons and concrete **bunkers** near the shore. Millions of mines were laid. Obstacles were built on the beaches, in the water, and farther inland where **paratroops** might land. By 1944, this "Atlantic Wall" stretched from northern Norway to the Spanish border. Troops and tanks protected it.

Germany's defenses extended well beyond the coast. U-boats, or submarines, patrolled the oceans for Allied invaders. The German navy also planted underwater bombs.

Some of the strongest defenses were along France's northern coast on the English Channel. German officials knew this was the easiest place for the Allies to invade. Across the narrow body of water, Britain was as little as 21 miles (34 kilometers) away.

Members of a U-boat crew look out over the water as the submarine leaves its base.

U.S. president Franklin Roosevelt (right) and British prime minister Winston Churchill (left) met several times to discuss war plans.

CHAPTER 2

Preparing for the Impossible

The United States joined the war in December 1941. Soon after, U.S. and British leaders met to discuss how to win the conflict. Some officials wanted to invade France as early as 1942. However, this action came with many challenges. In late 1941, the U.S. Army was not very strong yet. Also, new ships that could reach France's beaches had to be built. In total, it took more than two years to prepare for the invasion.

The United States, Great Britain, and other countries officially joined forces on January 1, 1942.

Choosing a Place and Time

The Americans hoped to invade France as early as 1942. Soviet leader Joseph Stalin agreed with their plan. The invasion would distract Germany and weaken its fight against the Soviet Union. But Allied resources were needed in the Mediterranean, North Africa, and the Atlantic Ocean. It was not until 1943 that they could begin preparing for a large invasion of France. Allied officials finally agreed on a time: the spring of 1944. They named the invasion Operation Overlord.

German forces had been in Soviet territory since June 1941.

German soldiers at Pas-de-Calais paint a white circle around their cannon for each Allied plane they've shot down.

When choosing where their troops should land, a place called Pas-de-Calais seemed the best option at first. It was close to both Britain and Germany. However, the coast farther south at Normandy offered more space and was less protected by the Germans. Normandy was also near France's two northern ports, which the Allies hoped to take from the Germans. In the end, Allied leaders decided Normandy was the place to go.

General Dwight Eisenhower (far left), Field Marshal Bernard Montgomery (far right), and other officials discuss the Normandy invasion.

A United Command

Allied officials formed a special group of military leaders to plan and command Operation Overlord. U.S. general Dwight Eisenhower was put in charge of the group. The others in the group were British leaders. Field Marshal Bernard Montgomery took over forces on land. Admiral Bertram Ramsay controlled naval forces, while Royal Air Force commander Trafford Leigh-Mallory was in charge of the air forces. Together, they planned what would become the largest military operation in history.

The French Resistance

Civilians in France also prepared for an Allied invasion. Many French people had already been fighting against German control of their country. These resistance fighters spied, destroyed German supplies, or **assassinated** German officials. However, their early efforts were disorganized. In 1940, the British Special Operations Executive (SOE) started helping organize French and other resistance groups. As the date for Operation Overlord came closer, the French Resistance and local SOE officials focused their efforts on preparing the way for the invasion.

Allied forces helped supply French resistance groups with guns, ammunition, and other items.

Gathering Forces

Before the invasion could take place, Allied troops had to gather in Britain. U.S. troops began arriving in 1942. By June 1944, roughly 2 million Americans had made the journey. There were also about 250,000 Canadian troops. They traveled overseas on large planes and ships. One of the largest troopships was the RMS *Queen Mary*. It had once been a luxury ocean liner. As a troopship, it could hold as many as 16,000 people.

The *Queen Mary* was nicknamed the Gray Ghost.

Almost 15,000 U.S. and Canadian troops wave good-bye from aboard the *Queen Mary* as they leave New York City.

18

The Fake First Army

The Allies wanted Germany to think they would land at Pas-de-Calais. This would make Germany move most of its troops there instead of to Normandy. So, the Allies created the fake First United States Army Group (FUSAG). FUSAG was supposedly stationed right across the English Channel from Pas-de-Calais. The Allies reported about FUSAG on the radio and in newspapers. They set up dummy tanks and planes. Germany was partially convinced. Even after the invasion of Normandy, Hitler expected an invasion at Pas-de-Calais.

Workers prepare to lay pipe along the English Channel as part of PLUTO.

PLUTO was the first underwater oil pipeline in the world.

Oil Under the Ocean

Tanks and other vehicles would go through a lot of fuel during Operation Overlord. Shipping the oil to France was risky. Ships could be sunk by German planes or U-boats, or by bad weather. To avoid this danger, the Allies built the Pipe Line Under the Ocean (PLUTO). Pump stations in Britain were disguised as barns, garages, and even an ice cream shop to prevent German planes from noticing and bombing them.

The Bombing Begins

Beginning in April 1944, to prepare for the invasion, British and U.S. planes bombed France to destroy German defenses. Targets included German military bases, **artillery** along the coast, and airfields. The Allies also bombed French railways and bridges that the Germans used to move troops and supplies. Many of the bombs fell in or around Normandy. But to confuse the Germans, bombers also targeted Pas-de-Calais and other locations.

An Allied bomber flies over France during a mission. Below it, smoke rises from areas that have been bombed.

21

Battle Supplies

D-Day is a term used to indicate the first day of an operation. In the days leading up to Operation Overlord's D-Day, the Allies made last-minute preparations. Troops gathered their gear. They received crisp, new uniforms and equipment. Much of what they carried was fairly standard, such as weapons and food. They also carried a few special items.

Extras

Each soldier carried extra socks, matches, candy bars, razor blades, and other items. No one knew when fresh supplies would be available again.

Rough Seas

Allied officials knew the journey over the English Channel would be rough. They supplied troops with anti-seasickness pills and vomit bags. Troops later reported that the pills didn't work. When the vomit bag supplies ran low, many soldiers ended up using their helmets instead.

Welcome to France

Soldiers were given French language guides and 200 francs, or French money. The francs had been printed in the United States but could still be used to buy things in France.

Reading Material

Troops also carried paperback books. These were much lighter and smaller than the hardback books usually found in bookstores before the war.

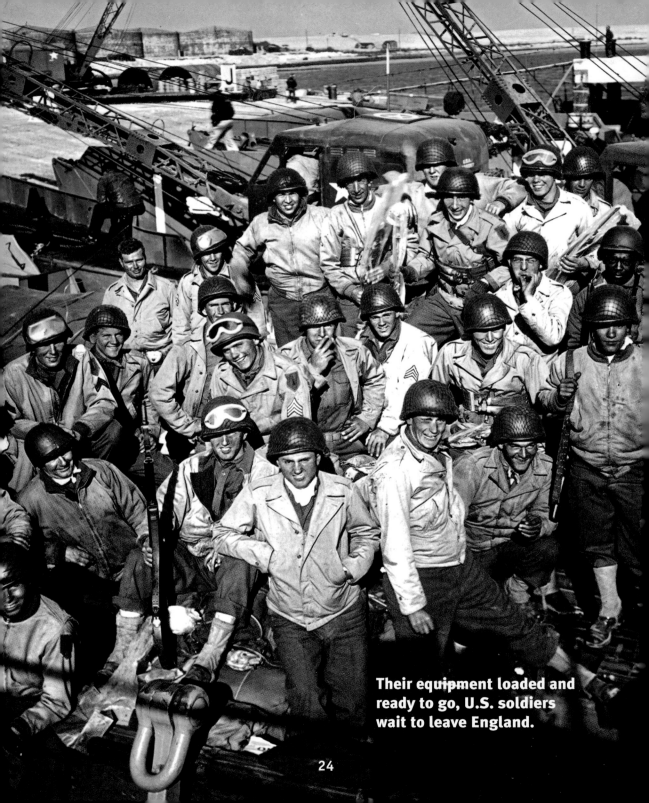

Their equipment loaded and ready to go, U.S. soldiers wait to leave England.

CHAPTER 3

D-Day Arrives

On May 31, 1944, special ships called mine-
sweepers began clearing paths across the English
Channel. They removed mines that might damage
the troopships coming on D-Day. At that point,
D-Day was scheduled for June 5. But General
Eisenhower delayed the invasion when a storm
blew up in the Channel on June 4. Everyone waited
for the sky to clear. On June 5, Eisenhower set the
invasion in motion again. June 6 became D-Day.

 Most of the invading forces did
not know their destination until
the day they left.

The Invasion Begins

Late on June 5, the first troops set off for Normandy. Paratroopers jumped out of large transport planes, and other troops flew in on gliders. They began landing behind the German line just after midnight on June 6. British glider troops took over a portion of German artillery and an important bridge. American paratroopers were unexpectedly scattered as they came in. However, they succeeded in confusing and distracting German troops in the area.

British gliders fly over Normandy, carrying supplies.

The Allied dummies dropped over France were nicknamed Ruperts.

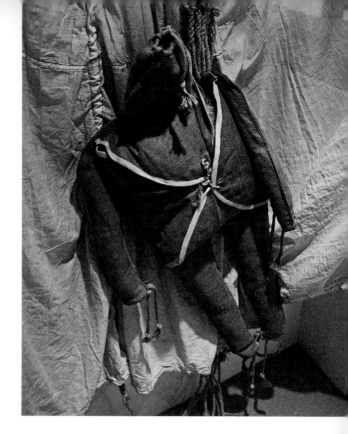

Other things that fell from the planes were intended to confuse the Germans. Near Pas-de-Calais, planes dropped pieces of aluminum foil. German **radar** noticed the foil pieces but could not tell what they were. Elsewhere, planes dropped dummies made of straw and canvas. This made it look like more Allied troops were landing over a larger area than they actually were.

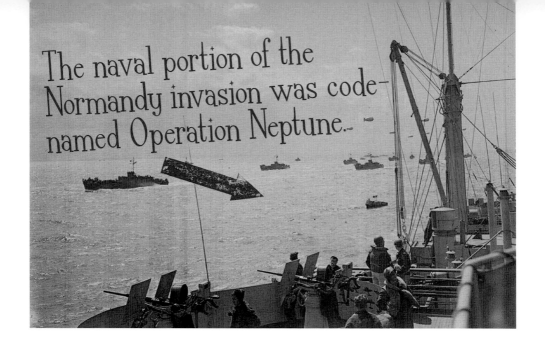

The naval portion of the Normandy invasion was code-named Operation Neptune.

Coming Ashore

The sun rose at 5:20 a.m. By then, Allied ships had arrived near the beaches. There were almost 7,000 ships in all, including landing craft and **merchant** ships. Many of them were large naval warships such as battleships and cruisers. These started firing at German artillery on the beaches at dawn. Fighter planes flew overhead to protect the ships. A total of about 156,000 Allied troops would land at Normandy that day.

Troops, tanks, and other equipment were brought in by ship. A few miles offshore, the men were loaded into smaller landing craft. These craft would take them to the beach. However, the Germans had placed large metal obstacles in the water. As a result, the landing craft could not get very close to the beach. Soldiers waded through water 4 feet (1.2 meters) deep or more. Some drowned under the weight of their gear.

The German obstacles along the beach at Normandy were simple but effective.

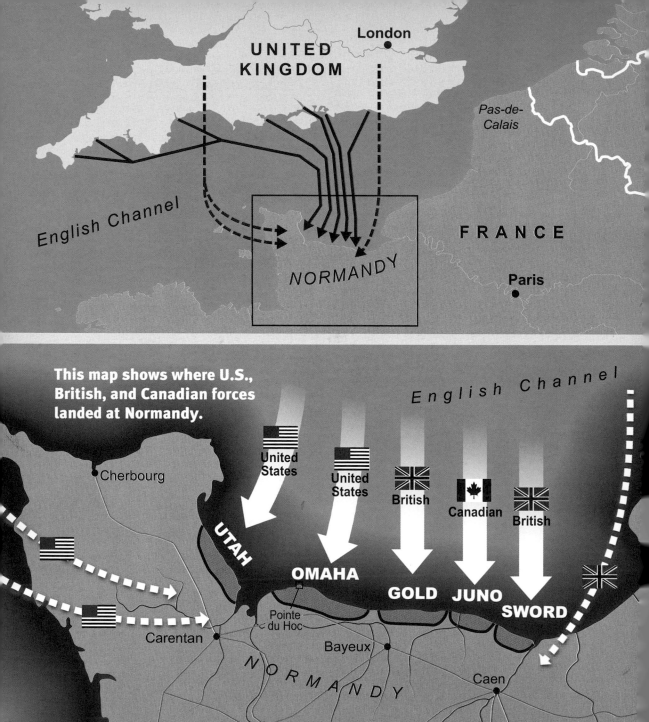

UNITED KINGDOM

London

Pas-de-Calais

English Channel

NORMANDY

FRANCE

Paris

This map shows where U.S., British, and Canadian forces landed at Normandy.

English Channel

Cherbourg

United States

United States

British

Canadian

British

UTAH

OMAHA

GOLD

JUNO

SWORD

Pointe du Hoc

Carentan

Bayeux

N O R M A N D Y

Caen

St.-Lo

Airborne Divisions

FRANCE

On the Beaches

Beach landings began at about 6:30 a.m. The troops were divided into five sections. There were two British sections, one Canadian section, and two American sections. Allied planners similarly divided Normandy into five sections. Each group of soldiers worked to take control of one section of beach. The British landed at two beaches, code-named Sword and Gold. The Canadians landed at Juno, in between them. To the west, the Americans landed at Utah and Omaha Beaches.

 The beaches ranged from 3 miles (5 km) to more than 6 miles (10 km) long.

Sword

Sword Beach was the farthest landing site to the east. There were fewer obstacles and fewer German troops there. Most of the Allied forces on Sword were able to get across the beach within a couple of hours. However, they did not get far before they were stopped by almost 100 German tanks. By the end of the day, the Allies were still stuck. They had suffered about 630 **casualties**.

Some troops carried fold-up bicycles, which few men actually used.

The first troops on Sword Beach included bagpiper Bill Millin (standing). He carried only his bagpipes, not a weapon.

Troops leave their boats and wade toward Juno Beach.

Juno

Beside Sword was Juno Beach. There, natural obstacles such as reefs made it difficult for landing craft to come very close to the beach. Mines also littered the coastline. Almost one-third of Juno's landing craft was damaged or destroyed. Troops had to wade through water that came up to their chests. Once on land, they came under heavy German fire. However, the Allies turned the tide by mid-morning. They suffered 1,200 casualties that day, but had reached farther inland than any other Allied force in Normandy.

Gold

The landing craft at Gold Beach also faced mines, and some craft were lost. However, other German defenses in the area were light. Several specialized tanks helped the Allies here and elsewhere. Some of the tanks were amphibious. They could float, using propellers to move through the water. Others had flamethrowers or rollers and chains that cleared out mines. The Allies there suffered about 400 casualties, which was fewer than many D-Day planners had expected.

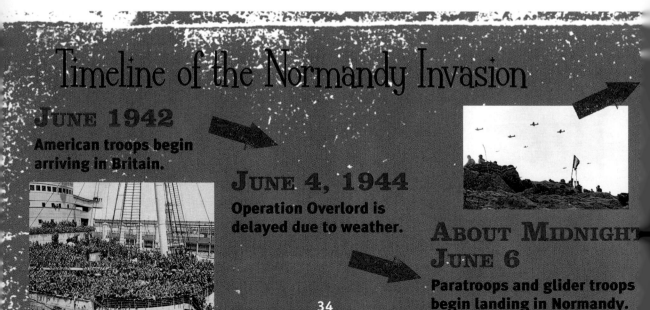

Timeline of the Normandy Invasion

JUNE 1942
American troops begin arriving in Britain.

JUNE 4, 1944
Operation Overlord is delayed due to weather.

ABOUT MIDNIGHT JUNE 6
Paratroops and glider troops begin landing in Normandy.

Utah

At Utah Beach, rough seas sent the landing craft off course, and mines destroyed most of the ships that were meant to give the craft directions. As a result, the troops landed more than 1 mile (1.6 km) from where they were supposed to be. The mistake actually worked in their favor. The spot where the Allies landed had fewer defenses than their original destination. In all, the Utah Beach troops suffered fewer than 300 casualties.

ABOUT 5:20 A.M.
Allied warships begin firing on German fortifications along the coast.

ABOUT 6:30 A.M.
Allied troops begin landing on Normandy's beaches.

JUNE 12
The Allies successfully link up to form one line across Normandy's beaches.

Soldiers in landing craft watch the action on shore as they near Omaha Beach.

Omaha

The Allied experience in Normandy was the worst at Omaha Beach. As at Utah, rolling seas sent the landing craft off course. Nearly all of the amphibious tanks coming with the troops sank. Cliffs and bluffs surrounded the beach. German gunners located along them shot at the troops in the boats, in the water, and on land. There was also a series of trenches from which German troops could attack the Allies.

Allied troops hid behind the Germans' obstacles on their way to the cliffs. They moved up the cliffs slowly, clearing out German troops as they went. By the end of D-Day, the Allies at Omaha had reached about 1 mile (1.6 km) into France with more than 2,000 casualties. One group of specially trained U.S. soldiers lost half their men while taking over a high cliff called Pointe du Hoc.

Wounded soldiers wait to be transported to a military hospital for treatment.

CHAPTER 5

Drive to Victory

The D-Day beach landings at Normandy were considered a great success, despite heavy losses at Juno and Omaha. By the end of D-Day, Allied soldiers had broken the Atlantic Wall and controlled all five beaches. The next part of Operation Overlord was to push across France and into the French capital, Paris.

Sainte-Mère-Église was the first French town freed by Allied troops during Operation Overlord.

Across France

The five Allied beaches managed to link up in one strong line by June 12. Some forces were able to move west and south. However, others were stopped from moving much farther inland. In northern France, high dirt walls, shrubs, and trees divided the fields. These slowed Allied troops and vehicles. At the same time, German tanks were moving in to block their way. It took about two months for the Allies to break through.

U.S. tanks move across a field in France in July 1944.

Hitler Must Die

With the Allies in France, several German officials
believed Germany could no longer win the war. They
wanted the war to end as quickly and peacefully
as possible. Hitler would never admit defeat, so
the officials decided to assassinate him. On July
20, 1944, they planted a bomb in a briefcase. Four
people died in the explosion, but Hitler survived. He
promptly arrested thousands of people involved in
the plot. Most of them were killed.

Parisians and U.S. soldiers talk happily outside Notre Dame Cathedral in Paris, France.

Freeing Paris

When the Allies broke through the German line in mid-August, the Germans decided to retreat. The bulk of the German army escaped northern France by heading east, into Belgium. Some German troops and officials remained in Paris. On August 19, French resisters began openly attacking the remaining Germans and taking over parts of the city. Allied forces entered Paris six days later. German forces in the city surrendered that afternoon.

Winning the War

Freeing Paris was an important step on the way to defeating Hitler. By September, Allied troops reached the German border. By December, they had freed most of France, Belgium, and the Netherlands. In April 1945, the Soviet army surrounded the German capital of Berlin from the east. Other Allied troops entered from the west. On April 30, Hitler killed himself. A week later, Germany surrendered. The war in Europe was over at last. ★

Soviet tanks and troops move through the streets of Berlin, Germany, at the end of World War II.

Number of Allied troops who landed on D-Day:
About 156,000

Number of U.S. troops who landed on D-Day:
73,000: 23,250 on Utah, 34,250 on Omaha, and 15,500 paratroops on various beaches

Number of British troops who landed on D-Day:
61,715: 24,970 on Gold, 28,845 on Sword, and 7,900 paratroops and glider troops on various beaches

Number of Canadian troops who landed on D-Day:
21,400, on Juno

Number of Allied casualties on D-Day: About 10,000

Number of German casualties on D-Day: Between 4,000 and 9,000

Did you find the truth?

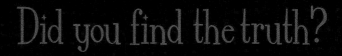

Some Allied troops carried bicycles when they invaded Normandy.

The invasion of Normandy began at noon on June 6, 1944.

Resources

Books

Martin, Martha Brack. *D-Day*. New York: Crabtree Publishing Company, 2012.

Stein, R. Conrad. *World War II*. New York: Children's Press, 2012.

Visit this Scholastic Web site for more information on D-Day:

www.factsfornow.scholastic.com

Enter the keyword **D-Day**

Important Words

artillery (ahr-TIL-ur-ee) — large, powerful guns that are used in warfare on land

assassinated (uh-SAS-uh-nate-id) — murdered someone who is well-known or important

bunkers (BUHNG-kurz) — underground or protected shelters, especially during wartime

casualties (KAZH-oo-uhl-teez) — people who are injured or killed in an accident, a natural disaster, or a war

concentration camps (kahn-sen-TRAY-shuhn KAMPS) — prisons where large numbers of people who are not soldiers are kept during a war and are usually forced to live in very bad conditions

fortifications (for-tuh-fih-KAY-shuhnz) — structures, such as walls or towers, that are built to protect a place

merchant (MUR-chuhnt) — a type of ship that carries goods for trade

paratroops (PAR-uh-troops) — soldiers who are trained to jump by parachute into battle

radar (RAY-dahr) — a way that ships and planes find solid objects by reflecting radio waves off them and by receiving the reflected waves

surrendered (suh-REN-durd) — gave up or stopped resisting someone or something

Index

Page numbers in **bold** indicate illustrations

About the Author

Peter Benoit is the author of dozens of books for Children's Press. He has written about American history, ancient civilizations, ecosystems, and more. Peter is also a historical reenactor, occasional tutor, and poet. He is a graduate of Skidmore College, with a degree in mathematics. He lives in Greenwich, New York.